HIS GRACE IN MY SUNSET YEARS

SAMUEL PATRO

Dedicated to

my revered parents

Late (Mr.) Nirmal Ch. Patro & Late (Mrs.) Premshila Patro

without whom I would not be what I am today.

❤❤❤

Contents

Foreword

I am honored and delighted to write this foreword for the book "*His Grace In My Sunset Years*", a life testimony and autobiography of my dear friend and former colleague, Mr. Samuel Patro. I have known Sam (Samuel Patro) for several decades, and we worked together for many years. He is one of the few YMCA professional secretaries I have encountered in my career who demonstrates such high Christian commitment and dedication to the YMCA mission. Through my long association with him, I can confidently say that his life has been like an open book or a burning candle, radiating light to those around him. I am certain this book will enlighten many young people who are struggling in darkness. Sam has enjoyed God's grace not only in his sunset years but throughout his life.

I first met Sam at an AOS conference, marking the beginning of a long-standing relationship. When he was the Assistant General Secretary of ISH London, I visited London while working in Sudan as the Director of the Refugee Service for the World Alliance. I still remember Sam warmly welcoming me at the airport and the memorable week we spent together. Later, we had the privilege of working together for about five years at the National Council HQ in New Delhi, where he was a key player on our staff team and a trustworthy colleague.

Sam was an active member of the Free Church on Parliament Street and a regular participant in the church choir. With his high Christian commitment and prayerful life, he has been a living witness of the Lord Jesus Christ. His deep faith in our Lord and Master guided him through the stresses and strains of life. He was firm in his convictions and gentle in his approach. His passion for Christian music, poetry, and writing devotional messages will always be remembered. His greatest contribution to the YMCA movement was in molding young leaders and in the extension and consolidation of the YMCA mission. I am sure this book is a living testimony of his life and mission. He regularly attended the annual fellowship meeting of the Retirees (IFYR), where his charming presence and devotional messages were very inspiring.

May God Almighty bless Sam and his family. Let this book be a useful tool for many young people to combat the evil trends of the present world. God bless.

T. Thomas
Former General Secretary
National Council of YMCAs of India

Exordium

It is an absolute delight, privilege, and honour, to write the exordium for *"His Grace In My Sunset Years"*, authored by Mr. Samuel Patro, whom I affectionately address as *"Raju Uncle"*! A man whom I have adored and admired for ages!

Having known him closely since my childhood, (early seventies), being an active member of Y.M.C.A., and part of Table Tennis Team & various Relief activities, when he was General Secretary, Cuttack Y.M.C.A., while his wife was my Teacher in school, in Class three and followed him through his stint at London, visited and enjoyed their magnanimous hospitality, hours of Scrabble, during his tenure at Y.M.C.A. Headquarters, New Delhi and after his retirement till date.

Words fail me, as I struggle to put adjectives on paper for such a God Fearing, God gifted, multifaceted, multitalented, amazing Human being, the most unassuming, simple, humble, uncontroversial Christian Leader, who practiced, what he preached, whose penchant for contributing biblical reflections, through his inimitable style of writing, be it songs, poems or books, has attracted a large following and tons of appreciation! Our deliberations would ultimately end up with *"Let's do something"*!

I really enjoy the brainstorming sessions at frequent intervals over various global issues besides Christianity, till date!

A voracious reader, prolific writer and dynamic, flamboyant Leader with extraordinary leadership skills, which were evident throughout his impeccable career, he never feared to take a stand alone! Not one, to sit quiet and take things easy, after retirement took up the mighty pen for God's Glory, to magnanimously enrich the world, sharing his vast knowledge, experience and blessings.

I cannot stop myself from quoting Robert Frost as an ode to his indomitable spirit:

"The woods are lovely, dark, and deep,
But I have promises to keep,
And miles to go before I sleep,
And miles to go before I sleep."

Solomon said, *"Of making books there is no end, and much study is wearisome to the flesh"* (Ecclesiastes 12:12).

However, not all books are the same. Some stand out, not as *"wearisome to the flesh"* but as lifting the spirit of the reader to heights of greater knowledge, wisdom, and faith regarding spiritual truth and "His Grace In My Sunset Years" is one such book.

It talks of God's immense infinite Grace even in the twilight years, beautifully, and I am sure, reading this glorious book will be a source of strength and blessing for many!

Ullas Pradhan
Ex – Visiting Faculty, Communicative English, Ravenshaw University, Cuttack, Non Executive Independent Director, Aesthetik Engineers Ltd, Kolkata, COO & Co-Founder, Sumato Futuristic Solutions, Pvt. Ltd. (DPIIT RECOGNISED STARTUP), Founder Director, SMART – EDGE Spoken English & P.D. Academy

Preface

"**His Grace in my Sunset Years**." – Does this caption sound odd? Was He not gracious at other times? The answer is – He is gracious and kind all the times. "*Through the Lord's mercies, we are not consumed, because His compassions fail not. They are new every morning.*"

We are living in a fast growing world. It is said – "*Children born after 1983 belong to the digital world. We are aliens.*"

In the midst of digital and technological progress, life becomes mundane and monotonous because of pressures from all quarters. Man has become lonely. There is a feeling of emptiness in his heart.

My focus in this book is to establish the truth that every moment of our journey depends on His kindness and manifold blessings. I have strongly felt His gracious presence in my life from my childhood and especially in my sunset years. My cup overflows. I offer my grateful thanks for His abiding presence.

The Author

Acknowledgements

I thank and praise Almighty God for His unrelenting grace to help me pen down my life's journey.

I would like to express my heartfelt gratitude to everyone who contributed to the creation of this book, "HIS GRACE IN MY SUNSET YEARS."

First and foremost, I want to thank T. Thomas, a colleague, a friend, and a well-wisher who has known me so well over the years. Your effort in writing the foreword for my book means more to me than words can express. I am deeply grateful for your support and encouragement.

To loving Ullash Pradhan, thank you for your beautiful endorsement of my book. Your words added a special touch and gave the book a sense of warmth and connection that only family can provide.

I also thank my beloved nephew, Chiradeep. Being the source my inspiration, your efforts in editing, formatting, designing the book cover, and getting this book published have been invaluable. Your meticulous attention to detail has made this book a reality.

I am also thankful to Soumendra Sahu for the DTP work. Your technical expertise ensured that the book was presented in the best possible way.

Lastly, to my beloved wife Aruna, my son Anurag, and my daughter-in-law Namrata, your immense support in everything I do has been a constant source of strength and inspiration. Your unwavering love and encouragement have made this journey possible, and I am forever thankful for your presence in my life.

The Author

My revered Dad, Late Mr. Nirmal Chandra Patro.

Author with wife Aruna, son Anurag and daughter-in-law Namrata.

ONE
FORMATIVE YEARS

The year was 1963. It was a stuffy and humid afternoon in Cuttack. I was in a melancholy mood. I just dropped my M.A. Final Year History paper as my answers were not up to my satisfaction. My mind was very unsettled because I would have to wait for one more year to write the exam. My room was quiet but there was a full-scale war in my mind regarding the uncertain future.

My uncle Hemanta Kumar Roul visited our home. I was summoned to meet him in person. He also heard about my unsuccessful attempt in the exam. He came with a specific proposal. During his discussion and talk he said, *"The Cuttack YMCA needs a young and energetic Secretary. Would you like to accept this post?"* He was actively associated with 'Y'. He gave me a graphic picture of this International Organization. I took time to decide. Meanwhile I read the available literature to know the history of this Organization.

Of course, I prayed for God's guidance to take right decision. My mom was a prayerful lady. She was also a great motivator and encourager. She advised me to accept this offer with faith and confidence. I also spent considerable time in prayer.

Few days later, I was mentally prepared to accept this offer. I met C.D. Jehasingh who was then the General Secretary of Cuttack YMCA. He was very friendly and jovial. He shared with me a brief history of World YMCA as well as the background of Cuttack YMCA. He posed a challenge that Cuttack 'Y' needed the service of a dedicated Christian young man specifically for the youth of Cuttack and the people of Orissa in general.

I returned home and spent a considerable time to take final decision. During our discourse, the General Secretary mentioned the motto of the YMCA- "THAT THEY ALL MAY BE ONE" (John 14:27). It was the High Priestly prayer of Jesus. The management of the YMCA is vested with the FULL MEMBERS (those who believe and accept Jesus Christ as their personal Saviour) but the general membership is open to all irrespective of their caste, creed and religion.

I joined the Cuttack YMCA as a trainee Secretary. My monthly stipend was Rs. 75/-. My first assignment was to look after the physical arrangement of a public meeting in the hall. Chairs were brought on hire from Kala Vikash Kendra. While returning the chairs, one chair was missing. Since it was my responsibility. I had to pay a partial amount towards the cost of the chair.

It was my first shock in relation to work ethics. I was dismayed and disillusioned. *"Is it the fate of a youth worker in a Christian Organization?"* But I realized later that God ordained that painful moment with His unrelenting grace and blessed assurance for my future journey. I accepted it.

My initial assignment was to organize Annual Membership Campaign to enroll more members, build up in house programme and meeting people. In spite of initial difficulties, I developed a liking towards my work.

With God's enabling grace, I was able to successfully complete my initial training for six months. The Board recommended my name for formal Secretarial Training in Bangalore. The National Training School was located in United Theological College campus in Bangalore.

Late Mr. R. J. Solomon was the Training Director. Though short in stature and physically weak, he was knowledgeable, witty, and full of vigour. He was a visionary in true sense. We were total seventeen trainers from various parts of India including one from England. My roommate was C.K. Rajan, a guy from Kerala. Rajan was a good Basket Ball player and a singer. Since I had a taste for singing, we became true friends. John from England was the only one overseas trainee in our batch.

We were assigned to various branches of YMCAs in Bangalore for group work. Conducting need-based programme for students, young people, families, church groups and occasional camping provided a base to acquire leadership qualities. We formed a good choir and sang in the Church Service and YMCA programme.

After completion of 10 months formal Secretarial Training at Bangalore I was certificated and joined back the Cuttack YMCA as a trained Secretary.

I returned to Cuttack with new zeal, vigour and enthusiasm to build up a strong YMCA with various developmental programme. But my dream was shattered. The hostel building was not fully complete. There was an outstanding bill amounting to approximately Rs. 30 lakh to be paid to the contractor towards building construction.

1964-1968 were the struggling years for us as our financial liabilities were increasing rapidly day by day.

Meanwhile my friend Nityananda Naik also joined the YMCA. We had a wonderful Board of Directors headed by Brig. Sangram Keshori Ray, a God fearing, daring, and committed Christian leader. We had to raise funds through special efforts. The Board members including the Professional Secretaries paid certain amount towards interest-free loan as a temporary measure to meet this financial crisis. One Christmas was a blue Christmas for us. We could not draw our salary, because of paucity of funds. Only support staff members were paid. But God's loving grace strengthened our faith to accept this difficult situation. Through these turbulent years God did not forsake us. We were able to clear all our outstanding debts in gradual manner.

Programme is the livewire of YMCA. We strengthened our base with meaningful programme activities, i.e., Physical Education activities (Badminton and Table Tennis). Including Literary Competitions, Toastmasters Club, Annual Prayer Week, Adult

Education in slum areas and Christmas celebrations.

The annual Christmas play staged at Nari Sangha Sadan was the most cherished event for the audience. Celebrities such as Samuel Sahu (Babi Bhai), Jharana Das, Himanshu Sabat, Dinesh Rout, Binoy Bhushan Dey, Sailendra Patra, Rajendra Sahu, Tapan Sabat, Madhuchanda (Chumki), and Arati Mohapatra participated in these plays.

Our Toastmasters Club has produced some top class Administrators, Educationists and Supreme Court Judges.

Camping was an interesting national programme at that time. On behalf of Cuttack YMCA I accompanied four boys from Stewart School, Cuttack, to attend the National Boys' Camp held at Nainital. Our accommodation was arranged at Nainital YMCA. G. W. Rowlston was the General Secretary and Basil Egbert was the secretary of Nainital YMCA. Mr. J. D. Martin, National Boys' Work Secretary was the Camp Director. Nainital at that time was a beautiful Hill Station surrounded by picturesque hills and beautiful lakes.

Cuttack YMCA had a property measuring about 15 acres of land at Bhagatpur. It was purchased by the National Council with a purpose to establish a Boys' Home. It was a big orchard full of cashew nut trees. A local resident was assigned to take care of the property. We also organized a Boys' Camp there.

Week of Prayer meetings were arranged in our YMCA compound and attended by many including our friends from other faiths. Many devotional and inspirational songs composed by me in Oriya were used during these meetings by our Choir. YMCA week of prayer was a real source of blessings for spiritual upliftment.

World Missionary John R. Mott once remarked *"YMCA is an outer courtyard of the church."* It is an infallible truth. YMCA has been playing a vital role as a bridge building factor between the church and community.

The YMCA President Brig. Sangram Keshari Ray was a committed leader. Almighty God used his leadership in a positive manner when the Cuttack YMCA was passing through a difficult time. In 1968, there was a communal riot in Cuttack. YMCA played a key role as a peace maker to establish peace and harmony under the leadership of Brig. Ray.

I still remember that incident. One afternoon, Brig. Ray came in his Jeep to our home and asked me to accompany him. A shop owned by a person belonging to a minority community was set fire by some hooligans. It was a well known shop. There was a big crowd. Brigadier got down from his jeep, I followed him. He had a fearless talk with both rival groups and advised them not to indulge in such inhumane activities. A Peace Committee was formed to find out a lasting solution.

YMCA established a cordial relationship with media sectors also. Dr. Radhanath Rath, Editor, the Samaj was a great friend of YMCA and extended fullest co-operation in providing emergency relief during natural disasters like flood, draught and cyclone.

C. D. Jebasingh, the General Secretary of Cuttack YMCA left Cuttack due to ill health. As per the decision of the Board I was appointed as the General Secretary.

After the sad demise of Brig. Ray, Dr. Sukumar Das became the President of Cuttack YMCA. He was also a Rotarian. His vast experience and able leadership helped the organization to make a steady growth in its development.

The year 1970 made a deep-water mark in the history of Cuttack YMCA. I was appointed as the Regional Secretary of the Eastern India Region comprising the states of Bihar, Bengal and Orissa. Nityanand was appointed as the General Secretary of Ranchi YMCA. Krupasindhu Moharana joined the Cuttack YMCA.

The year 1968 opened a new vista in my journey. My marriage took place in 14th May 1968. My wife Aruna is the only daughter of Late (Mr.) Sarasi Mohan Das, former Principal Stewart Science College, and Mrs. Saibalini Das. Her elder brother Asim Das was a lecturer in Statistics, Utkal University. His wife Mamata Das was also a lecturer in Home Science in Ramadevi Women's College, Bhubaneswar. Both were goldmedalists from Utkal University. Aruna's younger brother Susim Das, a Medical Doctor settled in

Khurda with his wife Sulata, son Sudip and daughter-in-law Nupur. Aruna served as a teacher in Stewart School, Cuttack. In my family, I am the only son of my parents. I have three sisters - Usha, Shanti, and Sandhya. They are married and settled in Cuttack, Jamshedpur and Balasore.

National Council of YMCAs purchased a flat in Cuttack on behalf of the Easter India Region. I started my office there. The nature of work from local to region was very different. My main focus was to visit the upcoming new YMCAs and strengthen the local units with leadership inputs as well as raising finances. Exploring the possibility of starting new YMCAs in unreached areas was a challenging experience. YMCA is a people-oriented organization and working with people groups is a blessed experience.

In the beginning of '70s, Cuttack and Bhubaneswar were the only established YMCAs in Orissa and Calcutta in West Bengal was the first established YMCA in India.

My role as Regional Secretary was tough and challenging. I had to work in close co-operation with the Regional Committee headed by the Regional Chairman and representatives of local YMCAs of the Region.

The Regional Committee decided to have a survey and concentrate on starting and strengthening new YMCAs in the following places on State basis: -

Odisha – Balasore, Berhampur, Jambu (Tankibelari), Jeypore, Mandapara, Phulbani, Rourkela and Raygada.

Bengal – Ranaghat, Ram Chandrapur.

Bihar – Patna, Marangada and Dhurba.

Regional Secretary's job involved regular visits and supervision. Every month, I had to stay out of home for minimum 10 to 15 days.

Life's journey is not smooth. Time plays a greater factor in determining the course of our journey.

Wise King Solomon says:

"Everything has its Time.
A time to be born and A time to die.

A time to weep, A time to laugh.
A time to gain, A time to lose.
A time to love, A time to hate...""

The year 1971 and 1972 made a deep impact on my life. It was a time of smile and tears, joy and sorrow.

Aruna was conceived. But it was a miscarriage. She was under medical care. Unfortunately, she lost her second child also. It was also a miscarriage in the advanced stage. Her condition was critical. But God was gracious to save her life.

When she had conception for the third time, Aruna was under high medication. Our son Anurag (Bitu) was born on 11th Jan, 1972.

Unprecedented disastrous cyclone ravaged the Eastern Coast of Odisha on 29th Oct. 1971. The sea became stormy and ferocious. Many coastal villages were swept away because of tidal waves. Hundreds of human lives were lost. More than ten thousand cattle were dead.

We immediately approached 'Y' care. 'Y' care is a London based Relief Organization. On our request the emergency relief materials were rushed. We formed a volunteer group and camped at Jambu (Tankibelari). The dead animals were being burnt by the side of the canal. It was a pitiable sight. On shift basis, we camped in Jambu village, for 5-6 months. A detailed survey was done in adjacent 10 villages to gather information regarding exact nature of loss. Livelihood of the villagers mainly depended on agriculture. Most of the villagers lost their precious wealth- cattle, as well as crops.

We carried out our relief programme in two phases- Emergency and Long-term relief.

Emergency relief included immediate supply of food grains and ration and the long term relief included the house repairs, renovation of wells, tanks and financial subsidy to procure agricultural implements and cattle.

The village councils were formed. The villagers were involved in planning process. Y Care, CASA and World Vision joined hands with us and we carried on this relief operation for about 6 months.

Gracious God heard our prayers and blessed our labour.

Normalcy returned after 6 to 8 months. Love, compassion and a sense of belonging cemented our bond of friendship with affected people in different villages.

Governor of Odisha convened a special meeting to recognize the services of the YMCA. It was also a great learning experience for me. Christ becomes very real when we become a part of the distressed and suffering community with his loving care and extend our helping hand with a smile.

In early January 1972, suddenly my mother's health deteriorated. She had the problem of indigestion and vomiting. She became very weak. After a medical checkup at home, it was diagnosed that she had cancer on her pancreas. This news totally shattered my dreams. I was totally broken. In my lonely room I cried aloud *"Lord, why me? Why did it happen to me?"*

Immediately I discussed with the Committee members and made arrangements to continue the relief program in my absence as I had to be with my mother. She was admitted in the hospital for surgery. The date was February 22. Since her admission I was spending time with her in the hospital.

The surgery was performed on 27 February. I went with my brother-in-law (my sister's husband) Sailendra early in the morning. Maa was calm and quiet. She asked me to read Psalm 90 before she was taken to OT. Unknowingly tears rolled down from my eyes in my prayer I begged the Lord to grant her His healing touch and give us grace to face this tragic situation. 4th March was mother's birthday. She completed 55 years that day. Dad visited hospital and spent considerable time with her. Some injections were not readily available in Cuttack. I took a letter from the medical authorities and proceeded to Calcutta to meet the Regional Manager of the Pharmaceutical company to procure the lifesaving drugs and injections. Post surgery period was very uncertain. It was a time of hope and despair. Sometimes she was normal and cheerful but suddenly her smile was turned to excessive pain and restlessness. Very often she needed blood transfusion because her platelet counts were unsteady and unstable.

My cousin Dr. Bimal Rath, then Associate Professor of Anesthesia was Mom's favorite and he was spending considerable time with her. He was also a great encourager. In his usual manner he was giving me hope that mom would return home soon but I knew her exact physical condition. As the days progressed mom's health was worsening from time to time. She was given blood transfusion but her feeble body could not accept it.

18th April morning was very dull and dry. Mom had light breakfast. Then she told me to read Psalm103. In her weak voice she recited the first verse. But it was very feeble and unclear. Then I committed her in prayer and asked God to fulfill His plan in mom's life. It was a very busy day in the hospital. Friends and relatives were visiting to pay respect. Her room seemed like an altar of whispering prayer. Dad visited mom in the evening but she became very quiet and silent. Dad left hospital with tearful eyes.

After some time suddenly she opened her eyes and gave me a blank look. I rushed to her with the hope that she would speak. She put her hand on my lap and tried to speak but could not. Then she closed her eyes forever. I expressed my sincere thanks to my dear friend Kartik, Rajat and my brother in law Shailendra for their tireless labour in the hospital.

It was past midnight. My most precious and ever-loving mother Premshila left for her eternal heavenly home where there is no night, no tear, and no pain.

My mother's death made a void in my life because she was my friend, philosopher, and guide. Her name was Premshila - an epitome of love. She justified her name because her love was so vibrant in her family, community, and church at large. I sincerely thank God for my mom and the impact she has made in shaping my life.

Expressing my emotions for my mother, I want to quote an acronym using the word "**MOTHER**," which is written as follows:

> *"M - Millions of things she has given me*
> *O - Only she is growing old*
> *T - Tears shed by her have saved me*
> *H - Her heart is as pure as gold*
> *E - Every moment with her is like heaven*
> *R - Reverence and respect she deserves"*

Our son Anurag (Bitu) was born on 11th January 1972, few months earlier to my mom's demise. He was a lovely and Smart child. But as he grew up we could detect that he was not attentive and responsive to our conversation and talk. Neither he could respond to any sound. We were sure that he had difficulty in hearing. We took him to ENT specialist for audiometry test. The test confirmed that Bitu had major hearing loss but it could be developed by using hearing aid and speech therapy.

I rebelled against God. I cried aloud and questioned Him- Why did it happen to me when others even without uttering His name are leading a happy and normal life. Why does He inflict such unbearable pain in His servant's life? This mental struggle continued for a longer period of time. But then I repented for my folly.

Aruna and I asked for God's forgiveness. Almighty God was gracious to change our mindset. We accepted Bitu as His wonderful gift and committed to give our best to improve his hearing.

We engaged a loving, caring and committed elderly lady to take care of Bittu as both of us had to remain absent from home because of our jobs. Her name was Basanti. She also hailed from a Christian family. We called her Basa Apa meaning sister Basanti. We are ever grateful for her loving care and service. With the help of a speech therapist Bitu was able to utter few alphabets and short words in Odia. The learning process was slow but steady. When Bitu attained seven years, he was admitted in a normal school where there was facility to integrate special children with normal children.

Bitu tried to cope up with the new study environment and showed some progress. We engaged a cycle rickshaw for Bitu. Sister

Basanti was daily accompanying Bitu with her to school and returning home with him after the school hour.

After proper counseling the speech therapist advised to help Bitu with hearing aid. It was useful to him in his studies, conversation, and interaction. He was also able to listen and to appreciate the music to certain extent gradually. He built up self- confidence to interact with his peer group including normal children.

Meanwhile, I attended the special meeting of Association of Secretaries held in Ceylon with my family. It was jointly organized by YMCAs of India and Ceylon. We had a wonderful stay at Colombo YMCA. Bitu also cultivated friendship with staff of Colombo YMCA and had an enjoyable stay.

When Bitu was 10, he asked for a bike to go to school. With much hesitation, we provided a bike. He fixed the mirrors at the front brake to have a clear view of the traffic from the back.

Gradually he was on his own and made the best use of his bike to attend the school. We praised God for his confidence and efforts.

In 1984 I got an invitation to attend the leadership development training program held at Haggai Institute, Singapore for four weeks.

I was granted permission to attend this training program. We were extremely fortunate to have Dr John Haggai with us in Singapore. Dr Haggai lost his only son when he was in his 20s because of the negligence and wrong treatment of the doctor. It was the saddest experience in his life but his undying and clear vision was praiseworthy. He made commitment to communicate the Gospel to the people in their own cultural context in Third World Countries. With this clear vision he established this training center. The training program included biblical interpretation, leadership, effective communication goal setting and writing skills.

Personally, I was blessed by the training and I applied these principles in my own work.

ᛈᛈᛈ

My Aunt, Late Mrs. Indumati Roul with Uncle, Late Mr. Hemant K Roul.

Our Training Batch with Director Late Mr. R.J. Solomon at Bangalore.

Honouring Mrs. Nandini Satpathy, then Chief Minister of Odisha

My Best Friend, Kartik Mohanty

Sisters and Brothers-in-law

TWO

APPOINTMENT IN INDIAN STUDENTS HOSTEL, LONDON

In December 1985 I received from the National General Secretary the letter of my appointment as the Assistant General Secretary of the YMCA Indian student hostel, London. By February 1986 I would report in London with my family. This appointment was for three years.

It was hectic time for us at home. I discussed this matter with dad and he was extremely glad regarding my appointment in London. He encouraged me to accept this new assignment. I was assured that my uncle's family would take care of him and he would have no problem. My sisters also promised to pay periodic visits.

We left for London in February 1986. Martin, one of our support staff of the hostel was present at Heathrow Airport to receive us. He was very jovial and friendly. Life in London was very different. The weather was mostly dull, drab, and grey. Roads were covered with ice. Woolen dress and special footwear were unavoidable. It took few weeks for us to acclimatize with local situation.

Our residential facilities were satisfactory. The hostel in Fitzroy Square, London, was like a mini-India, with its residents, food, and lifestyle fully reflecting Indian culture. Of course we had Irish, English, and Spanish working in our hostel as support staff. Joseph T Thomas was the General Secretary. Joy Spencer Singh joined us as program secretary.

I was in charge of hostel administration and Joy had special responsibility in our food services department. Our lunch service was very popular English people also developed a taste for Indian food i.e. rice, dal, sambar, vegetable curry, chicken curry, etc. The British Telecom, University of London and hospital complex were very near to our hostel. Our dining hall was always full during lunch hour with mostly English people employed in these institutions.

Aruna joined as the receptionist after proper training.

Brief History of the Hostel

Our hostel is situated at 41, Fitzroy Square. The nearest Metro station is Warren Street. The foundation stone of the project was laid by V.K Krishna Menon on the 5th of May 1950. But in the early years of 1920, the Indian YMCA was started in London when Mr. K.T. Paul and Dr. S.K. Dutta decided to start working with the Indian students. Dr Sarvapalli Radhakrisnan, who later became the President of the Republic in India was the Guest of Honour in the annual Dinner. During his speech he mentioned, "My first night in the country was spent in this YMCA. I felt that I moved from home to home." Mahatma Gandhi during his visit to London in connection with the first Round Table Conference also spent his first night in the Indian YMCA. Students, medical doctors, engineers and families from India and other countries enjoy their stay in our hostel.

Our Hall in the YMCA Indian Students Hostel has been named as, "Mahatma Gandhi Hall." Our Hostel is known as the Cultural Window of India. Most of our India Cricket Team members and celebrities of Indian Cinema had their occasional stay in our Hostel.

Bitu was admitted in a special school in Oak Lodge. Mr. Merrifield was the principal of Oak Lodge. It Was a Residential School. Therefore, Bitu had to stay there. Every weekend he used to visit us. Bitu picked up the sign language in English. Apart from regular studies, children were given practical training in other disciplines, i.e. swimming, horse riding and carpentry etc. Bitu was good in painting also.

After completion of one year, Bitu won an award in painting competition. The British Rail allowed our family free travel to any part of Britain. We visited Glasgow and Edinburg. It was indeed an unforgettable experience. Bitu was also good in Table Tennis and Badminton. He won the Table Tennis Tournament once organized by the London Hostel.

Our Hostel used to arrange coach trips to various tourist spots in London and other Suburban areas. We visited Buckingham Palace, London Zoo, London Tower, Canterbury Cathedral, Windsor Castle, Leicester, Bristol, Shakespear's hut and many other places. Madame Tussauds (Wax museam) made a lasting impression in my mind. This museum has unique seven zones and is home to over one hundred fifty incredebly life like wax figures from celebrities and Royal Family to cultural icons and music legends of past and present.

We had an opportunity to attend Dr. Billy Graham's crusade in London at Wimbley.

During our stay in London, my History Professor Dr. Manmath Nath Das who later became Vice-Chancellor of Utkal University stayed with us in our hostel for few months.

Every year our hostel gets official invitation from Buckingham Palace to attend Queen's Garden Party to celebrate Commonwealth Day. The Queen greets the audience with her magical smile and invites to join the Grand and lavish garden party. Some of our residents join us for this function.

We were regular visitors to India House to celebrate the Independence Day function on 15th August. Mr. J Alexander was the Indian High Commissioner in the year 1986. Lata Mangeshkar, the Nightingale of India was present that year as a special guest. We had a group photo with Lataji.

Every Sunday we used to attend church service at All Souls church which was very near to our hostel. Most of the worshippers were seniors. Youth was a minority in the church worship service but the Easter service and Christmas Carol singing was very lively with music and songs by the church choir.

We were invited to attend the AOS conference held at Glasgow, Scotland.

I was privileged to attend the European Secretaries Conference with our General Secretary held in Gwatt, Switzerland in 1988. We boarded the ship from Dover and reached Caleigh. From there we were picked up by a luxury bus to our destination. We halted at Paris and visited Eiffel Tower. The tower is made of 18000 iron pieces bolted together by 2.5 million rivets. When we arrived our Conference Center, we saw two other luxury buses in that campus. I was amazed to see this sight when the senior citizens both men and women in wheelchairs descended from the bus. Each wheelchair was carried by a young student. We were informed that these young boys and girls decided to spend part of their holidays with these elderly groups. What an encouraging and novel venture it was!

My son Bitu was also selected from his school to join a group to visit Interlaken in Switzerland sponsored by the Rotary Club. He stayed in Interlaken.

Truly, Switzerland is the Paradise on earth. The snow peaked blue mountains of Alps, green meadows and valleys, flower gardens, beautiful houses on the hill tops add to the idlylic scenic beauty of nature.

Our resident members used to decorate the hostel building with lights and organize the cultural function with music and dance during Diwali.

Christmas celebration was a unique program. Christmas dinner was being arranged for the resident members, invitees and dignitaries from the church and government. Indian ambassador Dr. Alexander and Mrs. Alexander, Arch Bishop of Canterbury, Dr Douglas Herd were some of the eminent guests who graced this Christmas get together.

Once a famous dance group from Odisha (Chau Dance) presented a program in our Mahatma Gandhi Hall. The audience was mesmerized with their highest standard of performing skill. Mr. M. S. Dalal, Managing Director of All India and Tata's ltd, the chairman of our Managing Committee was ably assisted by our dignitaries from various professions in London to look after the welfare of this prestigious Institution.

By the grace of God, I was able to successfully complete my tenure of service in London in 1989.

I received the communication From Mr. K. P. Phillip, National General Secretary to join the National Council New Delhi as the Secretary Extension and Development with an additional responsibility to coordinate the program activities in connection with the Centenary celebration of the National Council.

Bitu was very happy with his school and friend circle. Ruth and Geoff were his favorite teachers. They loved him as their own. Bitu was accorded a befitting farewell. As parents we both were invited to attend this function. Parting moments were full of emotion and tears. A beautiful farewell card was presented to Bitu on behalf of teachers and students with their signatures. Bitu's friends were drawn from various parts of the globe, i.e., Hong Kong, Singapore, London, Bangladesh and Africa. He was attending a special Christian Fellowship meeting. Bitu was very reluctant to leave London but after proper counseling he changed his mind. We were also given a befitting farewell in our hostel.

London depicted a curious mixture of cultural heritage. Asian community was emerging as prosperous business community. In every nook and corner in London you could find Tandoori Chicken. Well-known shops in Drummond Street and Oxford Street were owned by Asians.

In my final analysis, in our subcontinent India, in spite of cultural and religious differences there is an unseen power which has sustained this vast land and its countless people so far.

I LOVE MY INDIA. We left London in August 1989.

ᐅᐅᐅ

With Lata Ji on Independence Day 1968, at India House.

With Dr. J. Alexander, Indian Ambassador & Mrs. Alexander
in our Annual Christmas Dinner.

Family Photo of Secretarial Staff with in coming General
Secretary - K. Muthian and his wife.

A Happy Family - Secretarial Staff with Resident Members

Visit to Anne Hathaway Cottage (Wife of William Shakespeare)

A view of Odisha Chau Dance Performance
at Mahatma Gandhi Hall, ISH London.

THREE

APPOINTMENT IN NATIONAL COUNCIL, NEW DELHI

After our arrival at Delhi, we proceeded to our home at Cuttack. The atmosphere at home was electrifying. A rousing welcome was accorded to us. My dad was the happiest person on Earth. I hugged his frail body and could not check my tears of ecstatic joy.

During our stay at Cuttack, we met all relatives and friends after a long span of time. After a fortnight, we returned to Delhi. Our family accommodation in National Council campus was very comfortable.

When I joined the National Council, K. P. Philip was the National General Secretary and K. K. Jacob was the Finance Secretary. Bobby Samson was Secretary Youth Work and Christian Emphasis. Y. Moses was in charge of Human Resource Development and Manohar Sam substituted A. K. Choudhury as Secretary Records and Statistics.

I was accorded a warm welcome in the office by the NGS, all Secretaries and office staff. The working atmosphere in the office was very cordial and friendly.

My immediate assignment was to work out the program details relating to Centenary Celebrations of the National Council slated for 1991.

Compilation of Centenary History

Main features of the Centenary were publication of Centenary History, Souvenir, release of postal stamp and one day cover.

The inauguration of this festive event took place at YMCA, Madras. His grace Dr. Paulos Mar Gregorious, former President of the World Council of churches, delivered the key notes address and challenged the Y movement to determine its priorities as a change agent in the changing scenario of India. The most attractive program was the "Hallelujah" Chorus rendered by 100 youth voices. Youth choir was conducted by legendary Music Director Handel Manuel.

Dr. M. D. David, Professor of history and former Vice Principal of Wilson College, Bombay and former President of Bombay YMCA was requested to take up this responsible assignment of compiling the history. He did a magnificent job.

Isaac Jackson, Secretary Martandam, Rural Project and a gifted artist was assigned to prepare the logo of the proposed postal stamp and the front cover of the proposed Souvenir. He did a marvellous job.

We met the Registrar General of the Postal Division in Delhi, who was very excited as he had enjoyed a pleasant stay at our hostel in London during his overseas training. Although we submitted the necessary papers and the design for the postal stamp logo, there was a delay in obtaining permission due to his absence from the headquarters.

K.P. Philip, Y. Moses, HRD Secretary and I prayed for God's guidance and met the Prime Minister, P.V. Narasimha Rao in person with all necessary documents. He heard our petition and gave us the assurance to look to the matter.

Praise God. He heard our prayers. After two days of our meeting with the Prime Minister, I received a phone call from PM's office that our stamp was through. Our joy knew no bounds. We toiled day and night for release of stamp and centenary souvenir.

The theme of our Centenary Celebration was "PEACE FOR ALL."

After the completion of the formalities, the release dates for the postal stamp, centenary history book, and souvenir were fixed. We called on Vice-President of India, Dr. Shankar Dayal Sharma to request him to be our Chief Guest to grace the occasion and to release the Souvenir as well as the postal stamp and the first day cover. He also kindly agreed and we had this magnificent function in New Delhi YMCA.

To mark the Centenary, the National Council also organized national program for the Street Children. Nomenclature of street children was changed to *Junior Citizens.*"A junior citizen's life was totally transformed by education and he became a Police Sub-Inspector. With a grateful heart for the services of YMCA, he shared his testimony. Egbert Samraj succeeded K.P. Phillip as the National General Secretary for a brief period.

T. Thomas succeeded Egbert as National General Secretary. I had the opportunity to work with T. Thomas for a longer period. We had a cordial working relationship. The office staff members were also very friendly and hardworking. In course of time, K. K. Jacob also successfully completed his tenure of office as Finance Secretary. Isaac Judson joined his post.

As the Secretary Extension Development I had to co-ordinate the work of nine Regions in close co-operation with Regional Secretaries. For administrative convenience YMCAs in India were divided into following regions :

1. Eastern- (Bihar, Bengal and Odisha)
2. Western- (Gujurat, Maharastra and Goa)
3. North Eastern- (Meghalaya, Mizorm, Nagaland, Manipur and Arunachal Pradesh)
4. Central- Madhya Pradesh
5. Northern- Uttar Pradesh
6. South East – Andhra Pradesh

7. Southern- Tamil Nadu, Pondicherry
8. South Central- Karnataka
9. South Western- Kerala

During the Centenary Year more emphasis was given to start new YMCAs in the North Eeast regions. In Mizoram women took active part in formation of YMCA and its management.

For the first time, women were appointed as full time Secretaries in YMCAs in North Easturn Region.

Also, the National Council took up a project to have a survey to appoint at least 100 Secretaries in new unreached areas during the Centenary Year.

Even though tiring, meeting people and involvement in solving their problems in new areas was a great learning experience for me.

In 1992, there was a severe devastating earthquake in Uttrakashi which is situated in the foothills of Himalayas. Thousands of people were perished in landslide. The situation was very grim and dismal.

The YCare International, London immediately responded to our request and rushed financial assistance for emergency relief. I contacted Ramesh Paul, the General Secretary, Dehradun YMCA to assist me in the relief program and he gladly agreed.

After my arrival in Dehradun, we procured tarpaulin and other housing materials, medicines and dry foods and left for Uttarakhshi with a relief team.

In Uttarkashi we stayed at a Roman Catholic School. The Father and their staff were very friendly, gracious and kind. First day we visited the affected areas. It was extremely difficult to reach out to the people as most of the hilly areas were covered with Debris. Iron Bridge was squeezed like a match box because of the high velocity.

People were overjoyed and shouted in Hindi *"Fariste aa gaye"* (the angels have come). I did not have any idea of earthquake and its disastrous effects. It was a great learning and blessed experience. Perhaps we were the first to reach these unfortunate mass in the district. I thank God for giving me this opportunity to help meeting the needs of these unfortunate people through an organization like

YMCA.

After returning from London, my son Bitu was admitted in Ingraham Institute, Ghaziabad for a technical training for 1 year. After completion of the training, he joined St. Stephens Hospital, Delhi as a technician in Biomedical Engineering Department.

The year 1997 added untold blessings, joy and happiness to our family. Bitu's marriage was fixed. Aruna and I prayed for God's guidance to reveal His will to us.

Nagendra Pradhan and his wife Nihar Pradhan were residing in Kansbahal, Orissa. Nagendra was employed in L & T and Nihar was a teacher. Originally Nihar's family and my family had close contact as neighbours in Cuttack.

I wrote a letter to Nihar regarding Bitu's hearing difficulties and suggested to give their feedback regarding our proposal for Bitu's marriage with her daughter Namrata (Nicky).

Few dyas later we received a communication from Nihar regarding their willingness. We were overjoyed and thankful to our Lord for His wonderful plan.

Bitu and Nicky were joined together in the Holy matrimony in Cuttack Odia Baptist Church on 29th December in 1997.

After the wedding reception at Cuttack and other formalities we returned to Delhi. In Delhi also we arranged their wedding reception at National Council Complex.

After marriage Bitu was provided residential accommodation in St. Stephen's Hospital.

Bitu and Nicky shifted to St. Stephen's Campus after one month's stay with us.

I thank God for Nicky and her sincere support and cooperation to Bitu in every way possible. In course of time she also picked up sign language for better understanding and communication. Nicky was working with Schneider Electric India Pvt. Ltd.Being a normal person, she has mastered sign language in English and now she is an Indian Sign Language Interpretor, well versed in American as well as British Sign Language.

Bitu and Nicky began their journey with a positive note by putting their trust in God. Gracious God added His manifold blessings and has been guiding them till date in every possible manner. Praise God for His unrelenting grace and manifold blessings.

The year 1999 was again a tragic and sorrowful year for Odisha. The Super Cyclone hit the South East Coast of Odisha and adjacent areas. Crops were totally damaged. Loss of human lives as well as domesticated animals posed insurmountable problems for existence.

This news had international coverage also. Our overseas partner YCare International received SOS from the National Council for immediate relief as well as long term rehabilitation program. Immediately the action plan was prepared.

Dr. Christopher Beer, Director YCare International arrived Delhi and I escorted him to Odissa. We had a meeting with YMCA leaders in Cuttack and Bhubaneswar. Udipta Fullonton was appointed as YCare Coordinator in Odisha to carry out this cyclone relief program.

Extensive Relief Program was carried on in Cuttack, Bhubaneswar, Balasore, Mandapada and Berhampur with the help of local YMCAs. Udipta played a commendable role in this relief and rehabilitation programme.

My dad was aging. We were away from home for quite a long time. Of course I was in constant touch with him. It is a paradox that he could not visit us in Delhi inspite of our repeated request and persuasion. He was tall and thin but his mental agility was very strong. Memory was very sharp. His eyesight was perfect. He had no major health problem.

I had few years more for retirement. I opted for a transfer to Cuttack. The Committee considered my request and I was transferred to Cuttack as the Eastern India Regional Secretary with my pay protection. I was mentally prepared to accept this difficult decision. The National Council accorded a heartfelt farewell that left a lasting impression on me.

During our long stay at Delhi for almost 12 years, we did not miss home much because of our strong bond of love and affection with three families.

My cousin Anup Patro and his wife Subu were residing at Sansad Marg. Anup was the Auxiliary Secretary of the Bible Society of India.

My other cousin Squadron Leader (Retd.) Sachida Nanda Rath serving in the Leprosy Mission India completed his tenure as Deputy Director. His wife Priti Rath was the Principal of Ingraham Institute (technical department), Ghaziabad.

My other cousin Samuel Sahu and his wife Erica were residing along with their two children at Gurugram. They are still there.

We located a few families from Odisha and formed a fellowship with occasional prayer meetings and family get-together.

Aruna and I left for Cuttack. Bitu and Nicky continued their stay in Delhi.

ÞÞÞ

Meeting with Dr. Shankar Dayal Sharma, then Vice- President of India

Welcoming Dr. Shankar Dayal Sharma at the National Council Office.

At Centenary Thanks Giving Service at New Delhi YMCA.

Centenary History Book compiled by Dr. M.D.David

FOUR
HOME COMING

Home Sweet Home. After our absence from home for long fourteen years our return to Sutahat, Cuttack was replete with excitement and mixed feelings. Dad was extremely happy to receive us. So also the other family members. We were living as extended joint family. My nephew and his family were very loving, kind and affectionate. While we were in London they were taking care of my dad.

Our family atmosphere was fully activated with joy and laughter again after a long span of time. We had a family re-union with my sisters and other members.

I joined my office work. The Regional Committee extended a warm welcome. After a proper review of the Regional setup, the Committee decided to spend more time with the newly established YMCAs.

The YMCAs were identified as follows :

1. Orissa - Berhampur and Balasore. Initial visits were made to Raygada and Phulbani to explore possibilities of starting new YMCAs.

2. Bengal - Ramchandrapur

3. Bihar - Bokaro, Patna and Marangada in Ranchi. During my visit to Tankibelari YMCA once I came across a Boys Home in Chappali. The sight moved me deeply. I was reminded of those days in 1972 when we were tirelessly engaged in cyclone relief work. Miss Lily Quy, an overseas Missionary from London joined hands with us in

this venture. She used her Land Rover to carry the relief materials. Many children lost their parents. She had a vision to identify at least 10 boys to provide them shelter and education. Chappali Home is her dream child.

During this period a new door was opened for me. There was a request from the local Church to accept the responsibility of the church as its Secretary. It was a responsible task to manage the affairs of a big Church. I took time and prayerfully decided to shoulder this responsibility.

Almighty God granted his Grace and wisdom to guide me in taking the right decision. I praise God that His Spirit guided the Church Council in difficult situation and we were able to raise funds to complete the unfinished building of the Centenary Hall which was pending for a long time. We were able to build a local Church Prayer house in a rural village called Dandapdia. The main Church in Cuttack shared the major expenses and local people also rendered their voluntary labour in their church construction work.

I could complete my tenure in the Church with full satisfaction. I sincerely thank God for His able guidance and blessings.

My YMCA career came to an end in 2003. With profound joy and happiness I offered my gratitude to my Heavenly Father for his gracious presence and abiding love during my long journey with YMCA. I remembered His beautiful promise, "*I will instruct you and teach you in the way you should go, I will guide you with my eye.*" (Psalm 32:8)

After joining YMCA I was tempted to take up other alluring jobs for financial benefits but my mom's advise was "*If you have put your hands on the ploughshare, don't look back again*" I accepted her advise. My Heavenly Father never failed in keeping His promise to provide our needs.

The YMCA Movement in India bears a glorious testimony of countless men and leaders whose vision, commitment and trust in God have created history. Their unfailing enthusiasm will continue to inspire the present generation and the ones to come.

ᐅᐅᐅ

Eastern Regional Conference at Patna YMCA.

Eastern Regional Conference at Patna YMCA.

FIVE

POST RETIREMENT LIFE EXPERIENCE

Retirement with job satisfaction is a blessed experience. Many individuals are engaged in work day after day that is unsatisfying, unchallenging and without meaning. Here's a simple blueprint for a more satisfying life given by an eminent thinker and sociologist:

- Decide while others Delay
- Plan while others Play
- Prepare while others Daydream
- Learn while others Ignore
- Persist while others Quit
- Begin while others Stall
- Listen while others are Talking
- Advance while others Retreat
- Work while others pause
- Act while others Hesitate
- Believe while others Doubt
- Trust while others Vacillate
- Affirm while others Deny
- Venture while others Falter

Life became more tension-free, calm, and composed during this time. I started spending more time with my dad, and we grew close, almost like friends. He was a voracious reader, with a deep love for newspapers, religious books, and novels. Not only was he my best critic when it came to my writing, but he was also an avid bridge (card game) player.

I dedicated much of my time to writing articles for Oriya magazines and working on my new books. Invitations to speak at various churches and youth groups began to pour in, allowing me to share my thoughts on different topics in Cuttack, Bhubaneswar, and other places.

Every year, we made plans to visit Bitu and Nicky in Delhi, and we also took time to visit our sisters and other relatives.

We decided to establish a small Reading Room and Library in our home to honor the memory of my aunt, the late **Basumati Das**, who was my dad's eldest sister. To support this project, we advertised and asked for donations of old books, periodicals, and magazines. The response was incredibly encouraging.

The reading room and library was open to public in week days from 5:00 to 7:00 PM. This project was successfully managed for two years. Mrs. Santi Mohanty, Mrs. Swarna Mohanty, Dr. Shukalata Das were the pioneers of this noble project.

My cousin Pradip Patra was looking after this project on part time basis.

We also conducted Oratorial competitions on annual basis among the Christian youths and awarded cash prizes. The response was overwhelming

Pradip Mohanty was our close neighbor. He displayed his leadership qualities in YMCA on local, regional and national level. It is the most saddest experience that we lost Pradip in February and his dear son Anand in April 2021. God has granted his strength and courage to Pradip's wife Ruby to face this unprecedented tragedy in life. We also lost our good friend Nityanand Naik during this time.

On one occasion, the Cuttack YMCA arranged a special function to felicitate me and my colleague Nityananda Naik for our past services to YMCA. Our sincere thanks to Cuttack YMCA.

Dad was becoming weak because of his age. The year was 2008. One day he fell down from the bed. It was not very fatal but he was advised bed rest. Almost he was on bed over a week. I was spending time with him to give him company. May afternoon was very hot and humid. The date was 31 May. It was the last day of my dad's life on this earth.

He had a peaceful sleep in the morning but in the afternoon he was promoted to eternal heavenly sleep. I lost my father forever. I lost a person who caught my hand when I was about to fall in my childhood.

"Dads are most ordinary men turned by love into heroes, adventurers, storytellers and singers of song."

A grand burial was arranged in honor of his services to the community. His name was Nirmal meaning clear. He justified his name. He had a clarity of mind to understand the suffering and pain of the poor because he also struggled against many odds in his own life.

Praise the Lord for my lovely and Godly parents.

We were separated from Bitu and Nicky for over two decades as they were living in Delhi. We were praying for God's guidance to pave the way for both of them to come to Orissa. He heard our prayers. Bitu and Nicky came to Bhubaneswar in 2022. Bitu was posted in the Kim's hospital. Nicky is working in disability sector. They are residing in Nandan Vihar, Patia, Bhubaneswar.

ᐅᐅᐅ

SIX

PASSION FOR LITERATURE AND MUSIC

I had a natural inclination towards Odia literature from a very young age. I wrote my first song in Odia when I was studying in school. With lot of hesitation I showed this song to my cousin sister Shanti Lata Rout who was an approved radio singer. She was very happy and she encouraged me to write with confidence. It was a gift of God. I had to persevere to develop this talent.

When I was in college, God added his grace and blessed my efforts to pursue my literary skill. It was a gradual process. While working in the Cuttack YMCA, I composed many songs during the time of Annual YMCA week of prayer. Pradip Das and Purna Khuntiya composed the music. The songs were widely used in Churches and youth groups in Odisha. I also admire my departed friend Satya Sobhan Das of Balasore for his wonderful compsitions of devotional songs. The contributions of Pradip, Purna, Satya Sobhan and my cousin Lal Mohan Roul towards Odia Christian Music is invaluable.

In 2003, my nephew, Susanta Panda from Bangalore, produced a music cassette featuring my songs, which were well-received in the secular market.

I started writing features, stories and articles on various issues in our Christian magazines and contributed articles to newspaper on specific occasions like Christmas, New Year, Good Friday and Easter. My nephew Paresh Das of Bhubaneswar encouraged me in this venture. The appreciation and feedback from the readers enhanced my confidence and I was encouraged to improve my talent.

I was closely associated with the first Christian family magazine in Odia, "PRAVATI TARA" (Morning Star). Later, the magazine "AWHAN" (Challenge) was launched and gained equal acceptance among the people of Odisha.

In 1994 "Jesus" Film Project was launched all over India. It was dubbed in local Indian languages. For Odia language they needed my help. My friend Pradip Das requested me to accompany the team for script writing in Odia. It was totally a new experience for me. However, I prayed and took leave from office to proceed to Bangalore. A studio was hired for this purpose. We thank God that with His blessings we were able to successfully complete this task in scheduled time.

I praise God that He has blessed me with a gift of interpretation. My services were extensively used by Churches and youth organization to interpret the messages of speakers from English to Odia. I had the privilege of interpreting the messages of Brother D.G.S. Dinakaran, Rev. Ian North, Rev. Barry Moore, our good friend Prakash Yashudian, and many others.

Billy Graham Evangelistic Association launched a Good News project through satellite in Asiatic countries in the local languages. In India they needed the help of local interpreters in various states to translate the messages from English. I was asked to help interpret in Odia language. Pradip Das accompanied me to travel to Bombay. We stayed in YMCA. A studio was hired for this purpose. I was watching Billy Graham's message in TV and instantly rendering its odia version. Thank God for His amazing grace. We finished the program as per schedule.

Shakespeare said, *"Music when soft voices die, it vibrates in memory."* Music has been playing a vital role in my life's journey. Till date I have composed about 400 songs in Odia. Many devotional songs are being extensively used by churches and youth organizations in the state.

I wrote a ballad on the birth of Christ child. This musical program was telecast by Door Darshan.

A special song in YouTube on COVID was widely appreciated by the viewers. Subir Das and Nupur Das rendered their beautiful voice. I express my sincere thanks to both of them.

A volume of my literary works spanning over 60 years titled "SANCHAYITA" was released in the Cuttack YMCA in 2016.This book contains my songs, poems short stories articles essays and books. I express my gratitude to Odisha Evangelical Trust for its active support and cooperation in publishing this book.

In 2023, *"Fakir Mohan Sahitya Sansad"* (A secular Literary Forum) of Balasore, Odisha, celebrated its Seventy Fifth Anniveresary. I was invited and felicitated in this special function organised by this forum.

"Odia Christian Luminaries" is an inspiring narrative of the contributions and accomplishments made by few notable personalities to the Christian Community in Odisha in various fields. I praise God that my contribution has been duly recognised in this narrative.

ppp

Three Voices, One Harmony: Samuel, Purna & Pradip

Publication of Full-Life Study Bible in Oriya

Inauguration of Basumati Das Trust Library & Reading Room:
Chair Person, Shanti Mohanty.

Inauguration of Basumati Das Trust Library & Reading Room:
Prayer by Prof. D.K. Samantaray

Inauguration of Basumati Das Trust Library & Reading Room:
Praise & Worship.

Inauguration of Basumati Das Trust Library & Reading Room:
Address by Samuel Patro.

Launching of my Literary Collection, "Sanchayita"
at YMCA, Cuttack, on 30th September 2016

Sanchayita.

SEVEN
O LORD, HEAL ME

It was the cry of the Psalmist in his distress. The first wealth is health. All men were meant to be healthy and happy but suffering is a part of our existence.

Though I have gone through the path of suffering and near death experiences, the Heavenly Father has kindly protected me under His wings. Till date I have sustained seven surgeries on my body for various reasons. In 1976, I suffered from Neurofibroma. There was a growth in C3 and C 4 level on my spinal cord. It was not malignant but it compressed the spinal cord. I was not able to walk properly. My steps were imbalanced. It needed immediate surgery but before that the exact location of growth had to be identified. I was advised to have MRI which was a painful process. Surgery date was fixed. I was admitted in SCB Medical College Hospital. Dr. Sanatan Rath, an eminent Neurosurgeon, performed the surgery. It took about four hours. The growth was located in a very sensitive area of the spine. The surgery was successful.

It Is a paradox that the same growth appeared again on two occasions in a gap of 30 years. Second surgery was done in AIIMS in Delhi and the third in St Stephens Hospital, where my son Bitu was working. The third operation was done manually. One of my nerves was affected. Therefore I developed numbness in the right side of my body. Physiotherapy was done for a long time to activate the nerve system. My only prayer to Heavenly Father was to strengthen my right hand and fingers to hold the pen and write. He was gracious to hear my prayer. Even though my fingers in the right hand are still numb and weak but I am able to write. Apart from that I had cataract surgery twice. After a gap of few years I went through surgery again for removal of gallbladder stone and appendix. These painful experiences have increased my faith that our wonder working God is a great healer, sustainer and mighty saviour.

Healing means restoration of health. God is the healer. The Psalmist convicingly expresses his thoughts in these lines:

> "*Bless the Lord, O my soul,*
> *And forget not all His benefits:*
> *Who forgives all your iniquities,*
> *Who heals all your diseases.*"

Our healing depends on God's mercy.

ﭒﭒﭒ

EIGHT

OUR GREYING YEARS ARE GOLDEN YEARS

""Aging is not lost youth, but a new stage of opportunity and strength. The longer I live the more beautiful life becomes."

""Count your age by friends, not years. Count your life by smiles not tears."

In 2018, we celebrated the Golden Jubilee of our marriage. The function was held at Cuttack YMCA. Many of our family members, friends and well wishers attended this function. It was a time of joy and thanks giving for Almighty God's abiding presence and countless blessings in our life's journey.

Most of us are in our sunset years. But our greying years are the golden years. IFYR (India Fellowship of YMCA Retirees) is a glorious symbol of unbroken fellowship.

In most of the organizations members become disconnected and forget each other because of lack of communication and fellowship but for the YMCA movement it is totally a different mindset. We praise God for the vision of late Mr. D. S. Chinnadarai and other founding members who conceived the idea to create this fellowship. I sincerely thank God that due to His abiding grace Kurien Philip and I are alive today from our training batch to enjoy the Fellowship of this fraternity.

IFYR has strengthened our faith with confidence that we have not been defeated by age. We have to discover and deploy our talents.

"The God of Heaven will give us success" declares Nehemiah.

- At the age of eighty, Moses was called by God to accept the leadership to lead the nation of Israel.
- At age 81, Benjamin Franklin skillfully mediated between disagreeing factions at the US Constitutional Convention.
- At age of eighty, Winston Churchill returned to the House of Commons as a member of Parliament and also exhibited 62 of his paintings.
- At age 89, Michelangelo painted the inner roof Sistine Chapel and sculpted the figure of David in Florence.
- At age 87, Mother Teresa gladly served the poor and destitute in Kolkata.

Our fellowship transcends geographical barriers. When we receive a WhatsApp message from Rupert or from Keith in London, we are thrilled to get a feeling that we belong to a global family. WhatsApp messages with prayer requests from colleagues on occasions like birthdays, wedding anniversary or expression of sympathy during illness or bereavement give a sincere feeling that we belong to one family and we share our joy and sorrow together. I had the privilege to serve the IFYR as the Secretary in 2007-08. Egbert Samraj was the President.

"Rivers do not drink their own waters, trees do not eat their own fruit, the sun does not shine on itself and the flowers do not spread the fragrance for themselves. Living for others is a

rule of nature. We are all born to help each other no matter how difficult it is. Life is good when you are happy but much better when others are happy because of you."

- (Pope Francis)"

I would like to express my sincere feelings as a tribute to our wonderful fellowship in the following poem-

Unbeaten Greying Years

"Our greying years are Golden, a journey so adventurous.

With age we are not beaten for Emmanuel is with us.

Joys and Sorrows, Smiles and tears a mix of moments we have known.

They've made our journey challenging and yet pleasant as we've grown.

Our faith has increased steadily to fathom unknown paths ahead

and will never mind the future with countless blessings instead.

"Be brave and bold", the Lord does say, with promises that will last,

"I will never leave nor forsake you" because you're mine steadfast.

Bless the IFYR, O Lord, make our fellowship shine vibrant and bright.

Dispelling the darkness away with your everlasting in extinguishable light,

Our journey of faith must go on."

IFYR has completed its journey of 25 years in 2022. But this journey of faith must go on because God has strengthened this fellowship with His grace and mercy. We appreciate the present leadership of Stanley Karkeda as the President and John Verghese as the Secretary of IFYR.

Charlie Chaplin lived for 86 years. He said,

"If you see the moon, you will see the beauty of God, If you see the Sun, you will see the power of God, If you see a mirror, you will see God's best creation.

So believe it. We are all tourists. God is our travel agent who has already identified our routes, bookings and destination. Trust Him and enjoy life. Life is just a journey. Therefore, live today, Tomorrow may not be."

I am now nearing eighty four. My journey thus far has become a journey of faith, blessed by His grace. My heart is filled with gratitude for God's Protection, God's Provision and God's Presence. I am reminded of the inspiring words of an unknown author,

"I shall not mind the whiteness of my hair,
Or that slow steps faulter on the stair,
Or that young friends' hurry as they pass,
Or that strong image, greets me on the glass,
If I can feel as the roots feel in the sod
That I am growing old to bloom before the face of God."

ÞÞÞ

IFYR - 2008, Nagpur YMCA.

IFYR - 2009, Yelagiri.

IFYR - 2009, Yelagiri.

IFYR - Kochi, Ernakulam.

NINE
REFLECTION

Grace is a strong theme in the Bible. The word "*Grace*" is first found in Genesis 6:8 where it is written, "*But Noah found grace in the eyes of the Lord.*"

Grace means undeserved favour. Common grace of God includes prosperity, health, happiness, sun, rain, natural capacities, and gifts.

God's grace is abundant.

God's grace is all sufficient.

God's grace is glorious.

God's grace is great.

God's grace is manifold and rich.

We are living in dangerous times. Our world in the Twenty-first Century is crumbling in many spheres. Mankind is proud of its unprecedented progress in scientific and technological developments, but man has lost his identity in this colourful digital world. Man is devoid of humanism. Life has become self-centered, artificial, monotonous, and purposeless.

The first sentence of Charles Dickens' wonderful novel titled "*Tale of Two Cities*" begins with these lines: "*It was best of times; it was the worst of times.*" This remarkable expression is of greater significance in our present situation also.

Our daily newspapers, social media, and news channels present a vivid picture of a crumbling society. There's violence, killing, hatred, war, terrorism, corruption, communal disharmony, exploitation, human abuse and what not.

Human relationships are shrinking. Families are breaking up. Human values are substituted with unhealthy social status and ill-gotten wealth. In the midst of plenty, man has emptiness in his heart. But He is Emmanuel, God with us. His presence is the source of our joy and strength.

We as a family attend the Sunday afternoon Odia service at the Cuttack Odia Baptist Church. I also enjoy the fellowship of the English service on Sunday morning at the Mount House Church of God Congregation, Cuttack.

A news report indicates that by 2050, India will have a significantly older population, with the number of senior citizens at its peak due to increasing longevity. However, it is disheartening to note that many elderly people today are being mistreated or abandoned by their families and are residing in old age homes. Thankfully, "*Burning Lamp*," a Christian NGO in Kolkata founded by Rev. Sudipta Nanda, is dedicated to serving the elderly. This organization is dear to my heart. Recently, we have started a fellowship for senior citizens in our area also to support those who are needy and disadvantaged.

Most of our educated youth today are unemployed and under pressure. They are the victims of depression. Suicidal rates are fast increasing among the youths.

We have lost many of our dear ones during Covid-19. I too have lost some of my dear friends and feeling very lonely.

Today, on July 26th, 2024, I am nearing the completion of the final chapter of my book. This day also marks the inauguration of the Paris Olympics 2024. Interestingly, 45,000 security personnel have been deployed to counter potential terrorist threats. The world is currently gripped by fear and uncertainty. Yet, in these troubled times, we hear the gentle call of the Galilean: *"Hold my hand, come to me, I will give you rest."* This is Galilean's grace.

A man of God says, *"Much of our anxiety comes from living in the future. Likewise, much of our depression comes from living in the past."*

The Psalmist words remind us to live in the present. *"This is the day the Lord has made. Let us rejoice and be glad in it."* Psalm 118:24

Here are some guiding thoughts on living for today:

Just for today, I will count my blessings, not my burdens,

Just for today, I will change what can be changed.

Just for today, I will accept what can not be changed.

Just for today, I will reach out and touch someone with kindness and compassion.

Just for today, I will do something that I have been delaying.

Just for today, I will be optimistic and hopeful.

Just for today, I will live for these twenty-four hours and not worry about the future.

Our Gratitude should go hand in hand with His unrelenting Grace. *"Gratitude is the healthiest of all human emotions. The more you express gratitude for what you have, the more likely you will have even more to express gratitude for"* - Zig Ziglar.

Behind every sunset, there's a glorious and beautiful sunrise. There's no reason to despair.

CHRIST IN YOU – THE HOPE OF GLORY.

ᗡᗡᗡ

Home Sweet Home - Reminiscences

Bitu and Nicky with their Grandpa.

Family Get-together at Home, Sutahat.

Newly Wedded Bitu and Nicky with Bitu's friends

With Aruna's brothers and their families.

Anurag & Namrata with her Parents.

The Patras' at Sutahat